# Table of contents

Chapter 1: Entrepreneur defined

Chapter 2: Characteristics of successful entrepreneurs

Chapter 3: Entrepreneurial Orientation

Chapter 4: Success factors for SMEs

Chapter5: Research on SMEs Success in entreprenuers

Chapter 6: Reasons why many entrepreneurs fail

Chapter 7: Bowler and Dawood's characteristics

Chapter 8: Timmons' six dominant themes

Chapter 9: Types of entrepreneurship

Chapter 10: The entrepreneur's creed

Copyright 2014

Published by Liberty Chidziwa at Smashwords

Copyright 2014, Liberty Chidziwa

**Smash words edition**

**Smashwords Edition, licence Notes**

This eBook is licensed for your personal enjoyment only. The eBooks may not be resold or given away to other people. If you like to share this book with another person, please buy an additional one for each recipient. If you are reading this eBook and did not purchase it, or it was not purchased for your use only, then please return to your favourite eBook retailer and purchase your own copy. Thank you for respecting the hard work of this author

# Chapter 1: Entrepreneur defined

**Introduction**

Who are entrepreneurs? These are considered as individuals who have prepared to take enormous but , calculated risks, innovative in areas where most say that it cannot be done ,work long hours over extended periods of time that have resulted in them encountering personal problems all for the excitement of build an enterprise(Prince,2001).

In the early 20th century a Moravian-born economist writing in Vienna Joseph Schumpeter gave a definition of entrepreneur as the'' person who destroys the existing economic order by introducing new products and services, by creating new forms of organization or by exploiting new materials. He further supports his definition that this person is likely to accomplish the destruction by founding a new business but, there is a possibility to do so within an existing one'.

It is believed that they have a passion and bring a unusual concentrated effort to their projects often starting a business with nothing much beside an idea and go on to bring on board teams that have the ability ,the expertise and skills to utilized limited resources at their disposal to create successful business. Point to taken very serious by whoever intend to become an entrepreneur to accomplish success, that these individuals do not go into business because they have an idea or resources however, they invest their time and effort to engage in what is referred to as environmental scanning for viable business opportunities and take the initiative to craft something of value for gain (Kibas, 2000).

**Entrepreneurship defined?**

Entrepreneurship is a process which involves the creation of an innovative economic organization for the purpose of gain or growth under conditions of risk and uncertainty (Dollinger, 2001). It is a continuous process of creating something different of value to its users (Hisrich and Peters, 1992). The process is dynamic and leads to creation of wealth and economic empowerment to the in individual. The age in which we live has a referral as the entrepreneurship that is merely because due to estimation that many as 500 million persons worldwide either were directly involved in it or were trying to establish a new venture or were owner managers of new ventures that was during the year 2008.

Research in the areas of small business entrepreneurship has been identified as both a growing (Gibb, 1992; Gibb, 2000) and increasingly significant (Grant and Perren, 2002; Hisrich and Drnosek, 2002) area of academic movement and output. The academic discipline of Entrepreneurship and its related fields of Small Business Management and Business Innovation are currently catered for by over 50 journals. In addition, research into entrepreneurship draws upon many disciplinary foundations including: anthropology, economics, history, politics, sociology and geography (Curran and Blackburn, 2001: 123).

The growth in smaller entrepreneurial businesses enhances employment creation as young people generally obtain their first jobs with small firms (Barringer and Ireland, 2008: 19). Additionally, the development of small businesses that create products that can be exported enhances globalization. Furthermore, increased exports favorably affect the Balance of Payments of the countries. The innovations of entrepreneurial businesses also have a dramatic impact on society as a whole. New products and services improve the standard of living as well as the output. In addition to the impact that entrepreneurial businesses have on the economy and society, they also have a positive impact on the effectiveness of larger businesses. This is because many entrepreneurial businesses have built their entire business around producing products and services that help larger firms be more efficient and effective (Barringer and Ireland, 2008: 21).

Entrepreneurship has the following advantages: advancement of economic prosperity, combating unemployment, improved future perspectives and the advancement of own initiatives. The establishment of new business enterprises through entrepreneurship fuels economic prosperity and leads to job creation that combats unemployment. Additionally, the prospect of establishing a new business enterprise provides alternatives to job seeking individuals and could improve creativity and innovation through the advancement of their own initiatives (Marè, 1996: 9).

# Chapter 2: Characteristics of Successful Entrepreneurs

**Entrepreneurship further definitions**

Entrepreneurship can be traced back to the Austrian economist Schumpeter who argued that value creation was the fundamental role of entrepreneurs in a free market system and thus defined entrepreneurs as the individuals who exploit market opportunity through technical and/or organizational innovation (Schumpeter, 1934, cited by Turan and Kara, 2007).

Entrepreneurship is defined as the act and process by which societies, regions, organisations or individuals identify and pursue business opportunities to create wealth (George and Zahra, 2002). Harvard Business School provided a modified definition of entrepreneurship as "the pursuit of opportunity without regard to resources currently controlled" (Turan & Kara 2007). Nieman and Niewenhuizen (2009, p.9) define an entrepreneur "as a person who sees an opportunity in the market, gathers resources and creates and grows a business venture to meet these needs. He or she bears the risk of the venture and is rewarded with profit if it succeeds".

More contemporary research findings in this domain accentuate various elaborating and constructive inclusions in furthering the understanding of this construct, for instance: market-making, opportunity-finding and exploitation (Oksanen & Rilla 2009); firm level behaviour and entrepreneurial performance as well as entrepreneurial orientation and performance (Kreiser & Davis 2010); differentiating between founder and non-founder managerial capabilities (Langowitz & Allen 2010); as well the differentiating skills of the entrepreneur on a cognitive level (Duening 2010). An array of research papers have elaborated upon the correlation between culture and entrepreneurship, but little specifically providing evidence on the Indian entrepreneur in a South African context.

## Culture and Entrepreneurship

A variety of studies have lent support to the argument that cultural values influence entrepreneurial behaviour. The study of ethnic entrepreneurship and the importance of social embeddedness can be traced back to the works of Max Weber (1958) and Schumpeter (1934), both who argued that the source of entrepreneurial behaviour lay in the social structure of the societies and the value structures they produce (Urban, 2006).Weber (1956, cited by Turan & Kara (2007) indicate that entrepreneurship behaviour might be linked to cultural values and suggest that values and beliefs are factors that encourage entrepreneurship within certain cultural groups predisposing their members to entrepreneurship. Because individuals' personalities and behaviours, firms, political/legal systems, economic conditions, and social background are all intertwined with the national culture from which they originate the study of entrepreneurship under a cultural umbrella seems appropriate (Lee & Peterson, 2000). In a study relating to ethnic Entrepreneurship of Indian and Chinese immigrants in the US, Li (2007) concluded that one of the barriers experienced by the Chinese immigrants was the vast differences in culture. The American culture was so different from Chinese culture in many ways which resulted in a challenge for entrepreneurs to get accepted or trusted by native people. In case of failure the Chinese immigrants felt that their opportunities were limited due to not having much social and family support in the US. The Chinese entrepreneurs did find advantages in the US in that business failure is not a big deal in American culture, where as in Chinese culture failure is hard to deal with since the culture does not encourage risk-taking. The study concluded that culture was less of a perceived barrier among Indians. In a study relating to cultural values, market institutions and entrepreneurial potential comparing the US, Taiwan and Vietnam, Nguyen, Bryant, Rose, Tseng & Kapasuwan (2009) concluded that cultural factors appear to have a significant impact on people's desires to create new ventures and that people in a Western culture seems to have higher desires to create new ventures than those of Eastern cultures.

**Characteristics and attributes of Asian entrepreneurs:Past studies**

In a research for the thesis in the study of Asian entreprenuers ,the characteristics and sociological attributes that influence Asian entrepreneurs have been widely researched.Redding (1980, cited by Thomas & Mueller, 2000), suggest that unlike the idealised American entrepreneur characterised by the rugged individualism, there is growing evidence that the Asian entrepreneur relies on familial ties in developing their business. Morris and Schindehutte (2005) in a study that explored the entrepreneurial values and ethnic enterprise, an examination of six

subcultures pointed out that family and clan, hard work, loyalty, duty and relationships tend to be strong values in the Asian cultural context.Tsui-Auch (2005) points out that Chinese and Indian cultures are characterized by patrilineality, patriarchy and familialism. It is further suggested given the roots of strong kinship and communal networks one would expect that ethnic

businesses would maintain family management and avoid diversification into areas in which the family members did not have expertise. Abbey (2002) proposed that the cultural background of the entrepreneur plays a significant role in defining the motivation for entrepreneurship.

According to Basu and Altinay (2001) differences in financing a business influences entrepreneurial activity; for example, Islam prohibits usury; therefore one would expect Muslims not to borrow money from banks and would instead rely on savings or family funds. They also suggest that Muslims would not enter businesses that involved alcohol. Basu and Altinay (2001) also found that Indians who went to East Africa from Gujarat were mainly traders and hence it was not surprising that they engaged in trade enterprises in East Africa. A list of characteristics and attributes as described in the literature is provided below:

- Network of family and friends that are self-employed.
- Choice of trade influenced by parent's background and family tradition.
- Type of business influenced by cultural background.
- Sources of start-up finance (personal savings, Bank loans or family funds).
- Longevity of ethnic Indian traders in their specialisations.
- Values such as family clan, hard work, loyalty, duty and relationships tend to be strong.

Cultural factors are just one aspect that influences the entrepreneurial process. Another aspect is entrepreneurial orientation which is defined by Swierczek and Ha (2003) as a state of mind directing a person's attention towards a goal in order to achieve it.

# Chapter 3: Entrepreneurial Orientation

McGrath and MacMillan (2000, cited by Lumpkin, Cogliser & Schneider, 2009) suggest that successful firms attribute their success to having an Entrepreneurial Orientation (EO) approach to decision-making that draws on entrepreneurial skills and capabilities. This is achieved by keeping firms alert by making them aware of marketplace trends, new technologies and helping them evaluate new possibilities. Lumpkin and Dess (1996, cited by Lee & Peterson 2000) outline five dimensions of EO as consisting of autonomy, innovativeness, risk-taking, proactiveness and competitive aggressiveness. According to Lee and Peterson (2000) the five dimensions can be described as follows:

- *Autonomy* – the catalyst driving entrepreneurial activity is the independent spirit and freedom necessary to create a new venture. In order for the autonomy dimension to be strong, entrepreneurs must operate within cultures that promote entrepreneurs to act independently, to maintain personal control and to seek opportunities in the absence of societal constraints.
- *Innovation* – the creative processes of entrepreneurs will determine the strength of the innovativeness dimension of EO.
- *Risk-taking* – the willingness of entrepreneurs to assume risk. Individuals who are willing to accept the uncertainty and riskiness

*associated with being self-employed as opposed to settling for the refuge of jobs within organisations are often considered entrepreneurs.*

- ***Proactiveness** – is crucial to EO because it is concerned with the implementation stage of entrepreneurship. Proactive individuals do what is necessary to bring their concepts to fruition and gain an advantage by being the first to capitalise on new opportunities* (cited Lumpkin and Dess,1996).

- ***Competitiveness Aggressiveness** – an important component of EO because new ventures are more likely to fail than established businesses. An aggressive stance and intense competition are critical to the survival and success of new start-ups.*

Having reviewed the dimensions of culture and its impact on the entrepreneurial process relating to the skills and capabilities of the entrepreneur, the next aspect reviewed is the fit with SMEs.

### Importance of SMEs

A clear definition of SME as provided in the Namibian Ministry of Trade and industries, as amended in 2003, describes an SME as *"a separate and distinct entity including cooperative enterprises and non-governmental organisation managed by one owner or more, including its branches or subsidiaries if any, is predominantly carried on in any sector or sub-sector of the economy mentioned in the Schedule and which can be classified as a micro, a very small, a small or medium enterprise by satisfying the criteria mentioned in the Schedule"* (Government Gazette of Namibia, 2003).

SMEs are seen as playing an important role in the economies of many countries, thus governments throughout the world focus on the development of the SME sector to promote economic growth (Olawale & Garwe, 2010). According to the Ntsika Annual Review, in South Africa the SME sector form 97,5% of all business in South Africa. It generates 34,8% of gross domestic product (GDP) and contributes to 42,7% of the total salaries and wages paid in South Africa (Van Vuuren & Groenewald, 2007).

**Measuring success of SMEs**

There are several ways in which the success of SMEs can be defined. Lussier and Pfeifer (2001) suggest that small business success can be defined in the simplest terms as the ability to survive or to remain in business. Chivukula, Raman and Ramachandra (2009) suggest that entrepreneurial

success is defined using financial and non-financial measures. Financial measures are more widely used to measure success. In a study on the influence of socio-demographic factors on entrepreneurial attributes Chivukula *et al.* (2009) used growth in total sales and growth in employment as the financial measures in their study and non-financial measures of support received by the entrepreneur, work experience of the entrepreneur and involvement of the entrepreneur in the running of the business.

Walker and Brown (2004) suggest that not all business owners may want to grow their business. One reason for this is that employing staff and creating jobs for others as opposed to just themselves and immediate family was not an initial goal or motivation when starting the small business. Walker and Brown (2004) suggest that possible non-financial measures could be related to job satisfaction, greater independence, creating opportunities, encouraging new challenges and pursuing one's own interests are more difficult to quantify.

# Chapter 4: Success factors for SMEs

Delmar and Wiklund, 2008 (cited by Olawale & Garwe 2010) suggest that the business environment has a significant impact on the growth of a new small business. The business environment can be defined as all those variables both inside and outside the organisation that may influence the continued and successful existence of the organisation (Smit, Cronje, Brevis and Vrba, 2007 cited by Olawale *et al* 2010). The business environment can be divided into the internal and external environment. The internal environment consists of factors that are controllable by the business. The internal environment includes factors such as finance, managerial competency, location, investment in technology, cost of production and networking (Cassar, 2004, cited by Olawale *et al* 2010).

The external environment includes factors such as contractual and informational frameworks, macroeconomic and microeconomic environment, social factors (i.e. crime, corruption and ethics), technology and the regulatory environment (Olawale *et al* 2010). Some of the environmental factors that are perceived to be critical for small business success are outlined as follows:

❖ **Management skills**

Managerial competencies relate to the set of knowledge, skills, behaviours and attitudes that contribute to personal effectiveness and survival and growth of new SMEs (Hellriegel, Jackson, Slocum,

Staude, Amos, Klopper, Louw and Oosthuizen 2008, cited by Olawale *et al* 2010). According to Fuller-Love (2006) management development can be seen as improving the skills of managers in relation to finance, marketing, human resources, strategy, planning and operational management. The softer management skills relate to communication, decision-making and team building. Attahir (1995) suggests that management skills refer to the ability to develop and effect good business plans, to obtain and employ resources effectively, to balance obligations with business demand and to accurately keep records. Entrepreneurs are characterised by working hard for long hours. Pena (2002) found that entrepreneurs of growing firms are those that spend a large amount of hours (i.e. 50-60 hours) per week on business activities.

❖ **Marketing skills**

Marketing is often cited by researchers as a focus area for entrepreneurs (Hill, 2001). In review of the key characteristics of marketing management and competencies the author compiled the following characteristics:

- Vision
- Creativity
- Communication
- Motivation
- Innovation
- Intuition
- Adaptability
- Analytical abilities

- Judgement

Marketing factors also relate to the choice of location of the new business, understanding the market and size of the demand and the sales promotion skills of the entrepreneur (Attahir, 1995).

### ❖ Networks

According to Jack, Dodd and Anderson (2008) networks contribute to entrepreneurial capacity by extending the individual's asset base of human, social, market, financial and technical capacity.

### ❖ Level of education and training

The ability to compete is embedded in an individual's education which is related to knowledge, problem-solving skills, self-confidence and behaviour that allow entrepreneurs to identify and market opportunities and gather resources required to set up the new business (Rogerson, 2001; Martinez, Mora & Vila, 2007, cited by Kunene, 2008). The 2005 Global Entrepreneurial Monitor Report on South Africa concluded that the more educated a person, the more likely they are to start a business and the more people they are likely to employ. It further suggested that the potential of tertiary-educated adults to create employment is 2.5 times greater than for adults who have only completed secondary education.

### ❖ Access to finance and initial investments

The lack of capital and limited access to finance is a factor inhibiting entrepreneurship and influences growth negatively, as it impedes progress and

the timeous application of resources (Kunene, 2008).

❖ **Personal qualities**

Hills and La Forge (1992) cited entrepreneurial orientation as having six
dimensions as follows:

• The propensity to take risks

• A tendency to engage in strategic planning activities

• An ability to identify customer needs and wants

• A level of innovation

• The ability to persevere in making the vision of the business a reality; and • The ability to identify new opportunities. Entrepreneurship is not always seen as a desirable career choice and the factors that cause individuals to become entrepreneurs are termed 'push' or 'pull' factors. Push factor are "forcing" individuals to engage in self-employment, as where a more favourable condition is created by "pull" factors, meaning voluntary engagement evolves from opportunities in the market environment. Nieman and Nieuwenhuizen (2009) show the content of these factors:

• **Push factors**

- Unemployment

- Job insecurity

- Disagreement with management

- Not fitting in with the organisation

- The limitations of financial rewards

- Having no other alternative

• **Pull factors**

- Independence
- Achievement
- Recognition
- Personal development
- Personal wealth

• **Role models**

According to Nieman and Nieuwenhuizen (2009 p. 33) role models are defined as individuals who influence an entrepreneur's career choice and style, and include people such as parents, relatives or other entrepreneurs. Role models are about business owners sharing their practical experience and knowledge with learners and other new business owners (Auken, Fry and Stephens, 2006). Potential entrepreneurs are thought to develop an affinity for entrepreneurship through osmosis and absorb entrepreneurial knowledge that will become valuable when they enter the entrepreneurial world (Dyer, 1994, cited by Auken *et al.* 2006).

• **Experience**

The ability to assimilate experience and to learn from experience itself is one of the key factors influencing the entrepreneurial process (Deakins and Freel, 1998, cited by Kunene, 2008). Having professional experience in an organisation that is in the same industry as the one in which the entrepreneur starts his new venture can increase the probability of high performance and survival (Dahlqvist, Davidsson and Wiklund, 2000 cited by Kunene, 2008).

According to Nieman and Nieuwenhuizen (2009) entrepreneurs are more likely to succeed if they have work experience as they are likely to see entrepreneurial opportunities from an employment base. The above success factors outlined for small business success have been
identified as important in previous studies.

# Chapter5: Research on SMEs Success in entreprenuers

According to Attahir (1995) a study on critical success factors of South Pacific entrepreneurs resulted in the following factors being highly rated:

- Good management
- Access to finance and initial investment
- Personal qualities
- Satisfactory government support.

The study also pointed to the lack of management experience in the respondents surveyed as an explanation for the high ranking given to good management as a success factor. The findings of the study by Attahir (1995) observed differences in views between the entrepreneurs with and without formal education regarding the importance of three factors critical to small business success; namely, level of education, prior experience and personal qualities. Entrepreneurs in the study without formal education rated the mentioned factors more highly. In a study by Coy, Shipley and Omer (2007) on small business owners in Pakistan the study findings revealed that Pakistani business owners believed several factors contributed to their success and listed the following:

- Working hard for long hours
- Product quality
- Attention to customer needs

- Communication skills and interpersonal skills
- Business connections (networking)

Coy *et al.* (2007) point out that Pakistani small business owners strongly believed that business success lay within their internal control and business connections was the only factor rated representing an external factor for business success Entrepreneurs are viewed as being different from each other beside that there are certain characteristics that a person must have in order to differentiate him or her as an entrepreneur. Bear in mind that entrepreneurs are not born necessarily born with these characteristics however; they are acquired through life experiences and even through the entrepreneurial process itself. Not all of them have developed each of the following characteristics to the same degree, but they tend to have developed most them to some degree. What does it takes to become an entrepreneur ?Much research has gone trying to determine what type of people make good entrepreneurs because of diverse socities,diverse business opportunities . Never the less certain characteristics stand out and they summarized below.

- Be passionate about achieving their goals.
- Be goal oriented
- Be innovative ,creative and versatile
- Be willing to take initiative
- Have strong sense of commitment
- Have a strong need to achieve and seek personal accomplishment
- An eye for opportunity

The business environment today requires the development of creativity skills because entrepreneurial action is not necessarily intended for jobs that exist today but its focus is for future jobs and for business needed to create the jobs. The entrepreneur who understands the need for balance of analytical and creative processes will be much more competitive in the new and uncertain environments of today. The creative entrepreneur has the ability to navigate uncharted waters be will to anticipate change and create the future. One hurdle in developing creative entrepreneur is the false perception that creativity is a born trait rather than a developed skill. It is believed that everybody is capable of being creative; it is just a matter of how individuals develop that creativity within them to produce the most favorable results.

The issue of risk taking involves much more than just financial resources that will be lost when the venture fails inclusive it involve social and personal risks. All entrepreneurs are not immune to or may face personal risks because they might lose their valuable time with their family members. Liquidation can result in financial ruin which subsequently will result in social stigma associated with failure as well as the personal distress of letting investors down, employees, clients as well as their household members. To be one's boss is among the many factors outlined by a number of respondents that have driven to become entrepreneurs. Being tired to work for others give birth to new ventures instead of remaining employees they become employment creators an advantage to the alleviation of poverty , to reduce the unemployment rate in the country and lastly to boost the economic growth for the Namibian nation to become self-sustainable.

# Chapter 6: Reasons why many entrepreneurs fail

From the respondents feedback in past researches carried out it transpires that there are indeed many factors that attributed to some entrepreneurs not to have succeeded and eventually led to their exit barriers within the business world. One of the despondence observations was that frequently she saw many colleagues that are failing to succeed. The statement sounds very sad but indeed from a past dissertation by Wilfred ISAK in *A critical analysis into the success and failures of SMEs in Kansas region* is true that roughly 50% of small businesses in the great Kara's region have fallen in this down trap.

Bellow there are some personal reasons that resulted in a significant number of entrepreneurs failure. Each point will be discussed just to give an overview of research findings.

## Putting money first

The reason why many entrepreneurs fail is the love attachment to money. The desire to have their wallets loaded with cash has caused most entrepreneurs to divert from the business marketing concept that the quality of a business undertaking products or service is the most important than the money making concept. It should be noted as an important and essential point for entrepreneurs that have a dream to succeed and compete with their counterparts in other parts of the world to place the needs of customers first and have them in mind when taking any major steps. Customers are the lively blood of any business an appeal for entrepreneurs to adopt a customer centric approach.

**Lack of patience**

The late and most successful Jewish entrepreneur Mr. Harold Pupkewitz of Namibia has highlighted that many entrepreneur are displaying signs on impatient that after few weeks or months of starting a business closure will follow sooner than expected reasons be the love of money because they are claiming that returns on investment is low or perhaps results was not obtained. His thoughts was echoed by Mrs. Jansen of JJ based in Keetmanshoop in the southern part of Namibia enterprise that success is not a thing to be achieved overnight however, it is a practice that required continuous serious hardworking workforce, years of sacrifices, motivation thus the researchers appeal it is always very important for entrepreneurs to wait patiently for a business to yield results and not to be in a hurry and eventually kill your great dream because of slow results. Patients in whatever we do in life at the end of the day pays off.

**Failure to Network**

Taking the aspect of fierce competition among entrepreneurs many have opted not to form networking structures rather prefer to be alone. Many has alluded that as a factor that cause failing because when trying to increase your market growth ,size ,expand your geographic location that eventually lead to success as an entrepreneur the advice is not do underestimate the powers of others.

Those that have positioned themselves in the business fraternity have been preaching to young upcoming entrepreneurs to always try and associate themselves with top entrepreneurs and influencers in their field of business because you can tap into their audience. There are so many lessons entrepreneurs can learn from each other however, that decision is not imposed on them but is up to them to embrace this opportunity or not. Business networking aims are to create platforms for entrepreneurs to share ideas, learn from each other personal business experiences and in the ends their business will boom which also make their base for competition among foreign rivals tough making their entry barriers difficult.

**Failure to Plan ahead**

It was agreed by many of the respondents in previous researches that in order for success to be realized it is advisable for entrepreneurs to plan ahead ,visualize ,dream and strategist because, decisions taken today will determine the businesses existence in the long run. The advice to those entrepreneurs in the great Kara's region who are struggling to succeed be cautioned that when trying to invest or innovate as an entrepreneur is always important or advisable not to just come up with an idea and without having done further assessments go into the implementation stage that mistake will be costly in future in terms of monetary value and time so please fellow business man and woman think far more in advance words by a local business woman Miss.Justine. Do it right the first time.

I suggest to entrepreneurs from success perspective to be able to calculate what the future consequences would be in order to distiquish if the decision to be taken will be truly beneficial or not. Take note failure to plan is planning to fail.

**Failure to outline a priority list**

The final factor and also considered as a major element of entrepreneurial failure which is also has a referral as ''lack of organization'. It is an expected approach for every entrepreneur to prioritize and maintain a list of things that need to be done. Time is a factor that entrepreneurs should not take on time bear in mind that your competitors are watching your every move ,studying your products and services ,strategies on how to win your customers over so it is recommended to rather invest your time and effort on issues that matters that will attribute to survival and business growth. Everything in business might not work out perfectly no assurance is guaranteed ,but as ambitious and passionate entrepreneurs you must make sure you derived the best results out of things that will work out for you. Remember the definition of an entrepreneur given by Joseph Schumpeter as person who destroys the existing economic order by introducing new products and services, by creating new forms of organization or by exploiting new materials .He further support his definition that this person is likely to accomplish the destruction by founding a new business but, there is a possibility to do so within an existing one.

## Chapter 6: Traits necessary for a successful entrepreneur

### Introduction

Timmons (1999: 27) believes that the entrepreneurial leader should possess the characteristics to be able to inject imagination, motivation, commitment, passion, tenacity, integrity, teamwork and vision. He maintains that when they face dilemmas they are able to make decisions despite ambiguity and contradictions. Timmons

(1999: 28) continues that rarely is entrepreneurship a get-rich-quick situation; rather, it is a process of building, with continual renewal, which results in long-term value and a durable cash flow. In this chapter, traits of successful entrepreneurs will be analyzed by author and a theoretical list of traits will be developed from these authors.

## LAMBING AND KUEHL'S TRAITS FOR SUCCESSFUL ENTREPRENEURS

Apart from the traits of being a pharmacist, Lambing and Kuehl (1997: 12) suggest that the pharmacist will have to exhibit the traits of a successful entrepreneur namely:

- **A passion for the Business:** An entrepreneur needs to have a heart for the business, as there will be many hurdles and obstacles to overcome. If they do not have a passion for the business, it will not succeed.
- **Tenacity Despite Failure:** The entrepreneur must be tenacious in order to overcome the hurdles and obstacles that need to be overcome in order to succeed. Many successful entrepreneurs see failures as learning experiences.
- **Confidence:** Entrepreneurs need to have confidence in their abilities and, in particular, believe in their ability to accomplish their objectives.
- **Self-determination:** Authorities on entrepreneurship recognise the importance of self-determination and self-motivation in order to achieve success.
- **Management of Risk:** Generally public opinion is that entrepreneur's take high risks. This is not true.

Entrepreneurs see risk differently to others due to their detailed knowledge of their industry. This, according to Lambing and Kuehl (1997: 12), is seen as risks that are carefully calculated manoeuvres as opposed to random acts.

- **Changes are Opportunities:** Change is generally felt by the populace to be frightening and to be avoided if possible. Entrepreneurs view change as both necessary and normal. By exploiting change, the basis for innovation is established.

- **A tolerance for Ambiguity:** An entrepreneur has an existence that is much unstructured with no step-by-step process to follow in order to achieve success. In addition there is no guarantee of success.

- **Initiative and a Need for Achievement:** Successful entrepreneurs take the initiative where others may be reluctant to do so. Their high need for achievement leads them to act on their ideas and this need is motivation alone to achieve results from their accomplishments.

- **Detail-Orientation and Perfectionism:** Entrepreneurs often strive for excellence. This is a trait that that results in the attention to detail required in producing a quality product or service. This perfectionism is often a source of frustration for employees who may not share the entrepreneur's high need for perfection.

- **Perception of Passing Time:** Many entrepreneurs are aware that time is passing quickly and, as a result, often seems impatient to achieve the end product.

- **Creativity:** Success is often a result of entrepreneurs' ability to envisage alternative scenarios, often identifying opportunities that others fail to see. Successful entrepreneurs have an insight into what the customer wants and often have the ability to identify this want before the customer does.
- **The Big Picture:** Successful entrepreneurs have the ability to see the big picture when others only see constituent parts. They are able to scan the environment and evaluate it in order to formulate a bigger picture of the business activity as a greater whole.

# Chapter 7: Bowler and Dawood's characteristics for successful entrepreneurs

Bowler and Dawood (1996: 2) state that there are no stereotypes for an entrepreneur; however, entrepreneurs have demonstrated the following characteristics:· The fortitude or courage to continue despite challenges and obstacles; · The ability to cope in a dynamic environment;

The willingness to take risks when most other individuals hesitate;· The ability to identify business opportunities that cannot be seen by others.Bowler and Dawood (1996: 3) identified six misconceptions about entrepreneurs

These are:

- **Entrepreneurs are doers, not thinkers:** This is not true as, although entrepreneurs have a tendency towards action, they definitely think and plan their strategies.
- **Entrepreneurs are born, not made:** Research has found that entrepreneurial characteristics are not inborn.
- **Entrepreneurs are inventors:** Many entrepreneurs are indeed inventors, however, most entrepreneurs partake in other profit-making activities.
- **Entrepreneurs are academic underachievers:** Most studies on traditional business education had been slanted towards corporate business and not small business. Those involved in small businesses are more likely to specialise in his or her related field.

- **All a person needs to succeed is luck:** However, luck is enhanced through preparation to meet the opportunity.
- **Entrepreneurs strike success in their first business venture:** This is not true as many entrepreneurs experience a number of minor successes before they ultimately become successful.

## FOX AND MAAS'S CENTRAL CHARACTERISTICS OF SUCCESSFUL ENTREPRENEURS

Fox and Maas (1997: 12) state that the following characteristics have been identified as central to successful entrepreneurs:

- **Motivation:** People with high levels of motivation are those who are most likely to succeed as they overcome obstacles, maintain high standards and attempt to surpass others through performance-orientated goals. Performance and success are pursued for the feeling of personal achievement as opposed to either reputation or social identification. One of the most outstanding traits of the entrepreneur is the need to achieve. McClelland (1985: 254) found that despite the cultural differences between successful scientists, sports-stars, politicians and managers of large companies, there was a relationship between the need to succeed and entrepreneurship. There was also an improvement in the entrepreneur's performance after undergoing training in the field of achievement.

- **Drive, perseverance and energy:** These three characteristics are closely linked with motivation. They appear to be indistinguishable, but they all contribute to a positive personal orientation. Drive is the quality that individuals possess to enable them to work the long hours needed to overcome obstacles such as internal and external obstacles and fatigue. This high level of drive has been determined as to be indispensable for entrepreneurship.
- **Role orientation and purposiveness:** Entrepreneurs set specific goals for themselves that are in line with their objectives and not the problems they encounter on a daily basis. The objectives and direction of successful entrepreneurs assist in determining priorities and methods of performance measurement according to Fox and Maas (1997:12).
- **Time perspective:** Time is a valuable commodity to entrepreneurs and as such they regard it as extremely valuable. Tasks are thus future-oriented and finalised without procrastination or self-doubt.
- **Internal locus of control:** Internal locus of control is the belief in one's own abilities, not without making mistakes but within one's own limitations. Mistakes are seen as learning experiences and a successful entrepreneur is unlikely to repeat the mistake in the future. Those with an external locus of control believe that they are victims of fate.

They believe that circumstances beyond their control are responsible for either positive or negative circumstances.

> **Handling uncertainty:** Entrepreneurs operate in an uncertain environment. Their drive towards an end goal assists them when making decisions during periods of uncertainty.

> **Risk taking:** Common opinion is that entrepreneurs are gamblers. They are, in fact, not gamblers and make decisions based on qualification of the risk involved in starting a new project. There is also the psychological risk involved when decisions are required since failure could result in the loss of self-assurance and future motivation. The entrepreneur's reputation is also at risk according to Fox and Maas (1997: 14).

> **Confidence and self-image:** Research has shown that generally entrepreneurs have a high self-image. This is directly related to self-confidence as self-confidence combines with a number of other characteristics to result in self-image.

> **Creativity, innovative ability and vision:** This is directly related to the self-image of the person, their ability to have creative thoughts and the innovative qualities that are possessed when creating new enterprises. Training has been found to stimulate creativity, innovative ability and vision. Fox and Maas (1997: 14) state that the ability for foresight is termed vision and is that innate leadership quality that is

present, which is both appealing and daring and which is infectious. A focal point is established and acts as motivation for the entire entrepreneurial team when the entrepreneur has an artistic and precisely defined vision.

➤ **Ethics and integrity:** Successful entrepreneurs build their careers based on high ethical standards. This is due to the fact that integrity and reliability are some of the most important factors contributing to long-term success in entrepreneurial organizations. **Holistic approach:** An entrepreneur must be able to understand the effect of one event on the other elements of their business. The basis for this approach lies in sound conceptual skills.

➤ **Value system:** This is the ability to be more realistic about their own capabilities and objectives than others. Entrepreneurs are more prone to seek the advice of an expert than that of either family or friends. This is because they have the contacts required to exploit an opportunity. Networking is an important facet of an entrepreneur's life-style, since they would rather exploit an occasion than control resources. Optimism in uncertainty as well as belief in their own capabilities are factors, which lead entrepreneurs to success.

# Chapter 8: Timmons' six dominant themes

**Six Themes- Desirable and Acquirable Attitudes and Behaviours**
- Commitment and Determination Tenacity and decisiveness, able to
- decommit/commit quickly
- Discipline
- Persistence in solving problems
- Willingness to undertake personal sacrifice
- Total Immersion
- Leadership Self-starter; high standards but not perfectionist
- Team builder and hero maker: inspires others
- Treat others as you want to be treated
- Share the wealth with all the people who helped
- to create it
- Integrity and reliability: builder of trust;
- practices fairness
- Not a lone wolf
- Superior learner and teacher
- Patience and urgency
- Opportunity Obsession Having intimate knowledge of customer's needs
- Market driven
- Obsessed with value creation and enhancement

- Tolerance of Risk, Ambiguity, and Uncertainty Calculated risk taker
- Risk minimiser
- Risk sharer
- Manages paradoxes and contradictions
- Tolerance of uncertainty and lack of structure
- Tolerance of stress and conflict
- Ability to resolve problems and integrate solutions
- Creativity, Self-reliance, and Ability to Adapt Nonconventional, open minded, lateral thinker
- Restlessness with status quo
- Ability to adapt and change; creative
- problem solver
- Ability to learn quickly
- Lack of fear of failure
- Ability to conceptualise and helicopter mind
- Motivation to Excel Goal-and-results orientation; high but realistic goals
- Drive to achieve and grow
- Low need for status and power
- Interpersonally supporting (versus competitive)
- Awareness of weakness and strengths
- Having a perspective and sense of humour

Source: Adapted from Timmons (1999: 221)

Timmons (1999: 220) determined from a consensus of members of the Babson College's Academy of Distinguished Entrepreneurs that there are six dominant themes in the desirable and acquirable attitudes and behaviours for an entrepreneur. These are shown in the list above and discussed below:

**Commitment and determination:** These two factors were considered the most important of all the factors examined. An entrepreneur can overcome incredible obstacles and be able to compensate enormously for other weaknesses if there is commitment and determination. Carl Sontheimer, president and founder of Cuisinarts, Inc., is quoted in Timmons (1999: 220) as saying, "Entrepreneurs come in all flavours, personalities, degrees of ethics, but one thing they have in common is they never give up." Franklin P. Purdue, president of Purdue Farms, Inc., is quoted in the same text as saying that nothing, absolutely nothing, replaces the willingness to work. From this it can be seen that all entrepreneurial ventures require total commitment since, almost without exception, entrepreneurs live under constant pressure. This applies not only initially for the survival of the venture during the start-up phase but also for the perpetual growth of the enterprise firm. The new venture demands the highest priority from the entrepreneur's time, emotions and loyalty. The commitment and determination required is of a personal nature. The measurement of the entrepreneur's commitment is achieved by ascertaining the degree of willingness to invest a considerable portion of their net worth in the venture.

This might be achieved by being subjected to a cut in pay, major sacrifices in lifestyle and family circumstances. Timmons (1999: 220) is of the opinion that successful entrepreneurs who build new enterprises have the ability to overcome hurdles, solve problems and complete the assignment. They possess the characteristics of being disciplined, tenacious and persist in problem solving as well as the performance of other tasks. There is the ability to either commit or disengage rapidly. Difficult situations are not intimidating, to the contrary, they are of the opinion that the impossible just takes a little longer. An important factor is that they are neither aimless nor foolhardy in their relentless attack on a problem or obstacle that might be detrimental to their business. If it can be proven conclusively that a task is unsolvable, an entrepreneur will disengage before others. Although persistent, entrepreneurs are realistic in recognising their abilities and will obtain help to solve a very difficult but necessary task.

· **Leadership:** Successful entrepreneurs are experienced; this will include having an Intimate knowledge of the technology prevalent in their environment as well as within the Marketplace wherein they operate. They will have well developed management skills, together with a proven track record. As self-starters they will possess a high level of internal locus of control. Amongst the features of their leadership are their patience, the capability of installing tangible visions and the managing for the longer haul. At the same time as being a teacher, the entrepreneur is a learner and a doer whilst also being a visionary.

- **Opportunity obsession:**

Opportunity is the obsession of the successful entrepreneur. They are orientated to the goal of executing and pursuing the goal of accumulating resources. There is total immersion in the opportunity whilst still being discriminating, for at the same time they realize that ideas are plentiful. They are intimately familiar with their industries, customers and competitors. This obsession with opportunity is the guiding hand in the matter of how the entrepreneur deals with important issues. Timmons (1999: 223) points out that combination of the Chinese characters for crisis and problem means opportunity.

- **Tolerance of risk, ambiguity and uncertainty:** With the high rates of change and levels of risk, it is an accepted factor that there will be a high degree of ambiguity and uncertainty. It is the manner in which these people are able to manage the paradoxes and contradictions associated with this risk, ambiguity and uncertainty that produce the successful entrepreneur. Apart from money, the entrepreneur risks their own reputation. Therefore, the successful entrepreneur is not a gambler; rather they take calculated risks. Timmons (1999: 223) equates this risk with that of a parachutist. Prior to jumping from an aero plane the skydiver will calculate the risk involved and do everything possible to ensure that the odds are in their favor. In order to spread the risk, they get others involved in order to share the inherent financial and business risk. Both partners and investors have financial considerations and reputations at stake when they join with the entrepreneur. The creditors and customers who advance payment, together with the supplier who provides the credit, are at risk.

According to Timmons (1999: 223) entrepreneurs are comfortable with conflict and are
able to tolerate ambiguity and uncertainty. As opposed to a person working for a large conglomerate where their salary is guaranteed for the next several months, the start-up entrepreneur will face the exact opposite situation. There might be no income for several months in addition to the aggravating factor of the lack of organisation, structure and way of life. Every part of the enterprise is subjected to constant change, which introduces ambiguity and stress. There is no definition of jobs since their scope is continually changing. Both customers and co-workers are new and there is the inevitability of setbacks and surprises. There never seems to be enough time. Whilst maximising the good higher performance, which is due to the results of stress, they are able to minimize the negative reactions, which are the results of exhaustion and frustration.

· **Creativity, self-reliance and ability to adapt:** With the high levels of uncertainty and the very rapid rates of change that occur in new venture formation, an organization that can respond quickly and effectively is required. The belief in themselves is, according to Timmons (1999: 221), a characteristic of the successful entrepreneur. Any accomplishment or setback is within their own control and sphere of influence and they can ultimately affect the outcome. They possess the "helicopter mind" and are able to visualize panoramically from above and are able to view the problem dispassionately.

They are always dissatisfied with the existing conditions and are restless initiators. Effective entrepreneurs actively seek and take initiative. Willingly they place themselves in situations where they are personally responsible for the success or failure of the project. Where no leadership exists they will fill the vacuum. They like situations where the personal impact on problems can be measured. Within the context of the free market economy, the entrepreneur has historically been seen as an independent and highly self-reliant innovator and champion of the cause. Occasionally they have also been viewed as a villain. Successful entrepreneurs are adaptive, resilient and possess an insatiable desire to know how well they are performing. In order to determine how well they are doing and what is required to improve their performance, the entrepreneur will actively seek out and utilise feedback. This search and utilisation of feedback is central to the habit of learning from mistakes and setbacks and of being able to react to the unexpected. They are often described as excellent listeners and quick learners. Rather than the fear of failure, entrepreneurs are rather more intent on succeeding since they view success as being able to cover a multitude of blunders. The fear of failure, in the non-entrepreneurial mind is a factor, which will neutralise whatever achievement motivation they possess. It is this category of people who will engage in an easy task where there is little chance of failure or will attempt a difficult task if they are not held personally responsible if they do not succeed. Timmons (1999: 221) infers that the successful entrepreneur has the ability to utilise the failure experienced as a means of learning. They learn by being able to understand their own actions, the role-played by themselves as well as that played by others in the causing of the failure and how to avoid a similar situation or problem in the future. It is these successes and failures, which are an integral part of the learning process of the entrepreneur.

- **Motivation to excel:** Successful entrepreneurs have internal motivation to excel. This internal motivation appears to drive the entrepreneurs who are self-starters to compete against their own self-imposed standards and thus to pursue and attain challenging goals. Although there is this high motivation to excel, these entrepreneurs do not possess a high need for power and status. The personal motivation is from challenge and excitement of creating and building enterprises. Achievement is what is required to quench their thirst, rather than status or power. It is an ironical fact, however, that should their achievements be successful, power and status is gained as a result of their activities. By means of setting high but attainable goals, entrepreneurs are able to focus their energies, they are able to be selective in determining the priorities when presented with opportunities and they know when to decline an opportunity that they do not deem viable.

The possession of goals and directions helps to define priorities and provides a measure of how well the entrepreneur is performing. It provides an objective way of keeping score, such as changes in profits, sales or stock prices. Money is thus considered as a tooland a means of keeping score, rather than the object of the game. Timmons (1999: 223) asserts that the successful entrepreneur insists on the greatest personal standard of integrity and reliability. They are true to their word by ensuring that they do what they say and are deeply involved in their project. The high personal standards, which they set, are the glue and fibre that bind successful personal and business relationships.

The best entrepreneurs have a keen awareness of their own strengths and weaknesses and also of those of their partners as well as of the competition and other environments surrounding and influencing them. They are coldly realistic about what they can and cannot do and carry no delusion about themselves but, however, have a great belief in their own ability. Fate, luck or other external forces do not, in their view, govern the success or failure of a venture. It is by personal intervention that the outcome can be influenced. This attribute is also consistent with achievement motivation, which is the desire to take personal responsibility for the venture and exercise their self-confidence. Other valuable entrepreneurial traits are a sense of perspective and a sense of humor. It is the ability to maintain a sense of perspective and to be aware of both their strengths and weaknesses that makes it possible for an entrepreneur to laugh and hereby ease tensions. A sense of humour also frequently succeeds in getting a formerly unfavourable
situation set in a more profitable direction.

**Schools of entrepreneurship explained**

Cunningham and Lischeron (1991: 45-61) have categorised six schools of thought as regards to entrepreneurship according to various approaches and beliefs:

· The **"Great Person" School of Entrepreneurship:** Followers of this school support the idea that the successful entrepreneur is one with inborn abilities and traits such as intuition, vigor, energy, persistence and self-esteem.

· The **Psychological Characteristics School of Entrepreneurship:** Supporters of this approach regard the entrepreneur as one driven by a set of unique personal values, possessing a high need for achievement and with a special attitude towards the taking of risks.

· The **Classical School of Entrepreneurship:** Central to the characteristics of entrepreneurial behaviour is innovativeness, creativity and discovery, with the critical aspect of entrepreneurship as being in the process of doing rather than owning. ·

**The Management School of Entrepreneurship:** The devotees of this approach believe that entrepreneurs are people possessing the acquirable skills of planning, organising and managing business ownership and risk taking.

· The **Leadership School of Entrepreneurship:** Supporters of this approach regard the entrepreneur as one with the ability to motivate, direct and lead other people. They are also able to achieve their objectives through the positive reactions of those around them.

- The **Intrapreneurship School of Entrepreneurship:** The Intrapreneur is seen as an alert and innovative employee who possesses and utilizes entrepreneurial skills and attributes within an organisation in order to develop new and/or improved products, markets and methods to further the goals and objectives of the organisation.

# Chapter 9: Types of entrepreneurship

Milner (1996: 4) is of the opinion that there are four distinct types of entrepreneurs

Namely:

The **Personal Achiever:** This describes the classic entrepreneur who spends long hours at work, is full of energy, thrives on feedback as regards to their performance, enjoys planning and setting goals for future achievements. This type of entrepreneur has initiative as well as commitment to their organisation. They have a strong internal locus of control and are guided by their own goals, not those of others. Constantly putting out fires and continually dealing with crises they achieve success. They wear many hats depending upon which crisis predominates at the time. An attempt is made to be good at everything;

**The Super salesperson:** This individual possesses empathy for others and attempts to be of service at all times. They utilise a soft-sell approach and are rewarded by sales from their customers' desire to reciprocate. Relationships are of paramount importance to the salesperson and them like social situations and groups.

**The Real Manager:** They are effective in corporate leadership positions since they desire to take charge. A positive disposal to authority is displayed and they enjoy power and acting a part. The entry into entrepreneurship is often from larger firms. As entrepreneurs, they frequently become capable marketers, either by utilizing the marketing process or as efficient salespeople. By the use of logic and forceful persuasion, customers are managed into a sale. This approach is different to that of the super salesperson. Their power guides ventures into major growth. There is no need for a general manager since they are the general manager. Success is achieved via the

Managing Route: here they find or begin a business of sufficient size, which requires their managerial skills;

**The Expert Idea Generator:** This type of person is involved with the invention of new products, finding a new niche for existing products, developing new processes and thereby creating a competitive edge over business rivals. The downfall of this type of entrepreneur is that they are often carried away with enthusiasm and fail to take sufficient care when calculating risk. They tend to be idealistic.

From a study undertaken by the University of Land in Sweden, Kroon and Moolman

(1991: 10-12) have enlarged the classification into the following types:

· **Intrapreneurs:** These are employees of an organisation who display entrepreneurial

talents by initiating innovation and undertaking calculated risks within the organisation.

· **Expreneurs:** Whilst in the employ of another, they detect an opportunity and go out and start a new independent business.

**Novopreneurs:** The innovators and inventors of unique products and services.

**Interpreneurs:** By amalgamating several small businesses, a large highly profit orientated business is created by this type of entrepreneur.

**Renovateurs:** This type of entrepreneur, as the name suggests, takes stagnant or failing enterprises and resuscitates them. The actions taken are often extreme and affect

the present staff, operating procedures and policies.

## Desirable but not acquirable attitudes and behaviours

There is a further list of characteristics which, according to Timmons (1999: 225), are more innate than acquired. This is fortunately a much shorter list and there is some degree of argument as to whether these characteristics can be nurtured or learnt.

**Energy, health and emotional stability:** The extraordinary workloads and the stressful demands, which are placed on the entrepreneur, demand a premium when energy, physical and emotional health is considered. Genetics plays an important part in the make-up of the individual, but careful attention to eating, drinking habits, exercise and relaxation helps to fine-tune the genetic attributes.

· **Creativity and innovativeness:** Initially creativity was considered to be an exclusively inherited capacity and although genetics plays a great part in the level of creativity and innovativeness, it is not the only factor.

**Intelligence:** Intelligence and conceptual ability are great advantages for an entrepreneur. It is highly unlikely that the founder of any successful higher potential venture could be classed as being either dumb or having an average intelligence. The school dropouts who go on to become truly extraordinary entrepreneurs are those who are street-wise (having a nose for business), possessing the entrepreneur's gut feel and instincts. They have a special type of intelligence.

**Capacity to inspire:** Vision is that natural leadership quality that is charismatic, bold and inspirational. As great leaders share their visions, so do many of the truly extraordinary entrepreneurs. It is difficult to argue that such exceptional personal qualities are other than inborn. However, although an entrepreneur's charisma quotient might be low, they are still leaders with their own type of leadership characteristics. The entrepreneur's goals and values will establish the atmosphere within which all subsequent activity will unfold and the inspiration of the entrepreneur, regardless of the form, whichit takes, will shape the future venture.

**Values:** The personal and ethical values of the entrepreneur seem to be reflected by the environment and background from which they come. These values are developed early in life and are an integral part of an individual.

## Chapter 10: The entrepreneur's creed

Timmons (1999: 228) has developed an entrepreneur's creed since so much time and space would not have been spent on the entrepreneurial mind if it were just of academic interest. Entrepreneurs, when interviewed and asked to complete open-ended questions about what they considered the most critical concepts, skills, and knowledge required for running a business, both today and in five years' time, were most revealing in their answers. Most mentioned mental attitudes and philosophies which were based on entrepreneurial attributes, as opposed to specific skills or organisational concepts. The answers, which were gathered together, produced what has been called an entrepreneur's creed.

- Do what gives you energy - have fun;
- Figure out how to make it work;
- Say, "can do," rather than "cannot" or "maybe";
- Tenacity and creativity will triumph;
- Anything is possible if you believe you can do it;
- If you do not know it cannot be done, then you will go ahead and do it;
- The cup is half-full, not half-empty;
- Be dissatisfied with the way things are - and look for improvement;
- Do things differently;

- Do not take a risk if you do not have to - but take a calculated risk if it is the right opportunity for you;

- Businesses fail; successful entrepreneurs learn - but keep the tuition low;
- It is easier to beg for forgiveness than to ask for permission in the first place;
- Make opportunity and results your obsession - not money;
- Money is a tool and a scorecard available to the right people with the right opportunity at the right time;
- Making money is even more fun than spending it;
- Make heroes out of others - a team builds a business; an individual makes a living;
- Take pride in your accomplishments - it is contagious;

**Bibliography**

Altink, W.M.M., Born, M.Ph. & de Wilde, G.H. (1989), *Beoordeling van startende ondernemers: Handleiding bij de beoordelingsschaal voor ondernemerskwaliteiten (BSOK)*, Instituut Midden en Kleinbedrijf, Hoofddorp.

Audretsch, D.B. & Thurik, A.R. (2000), Capitalism and democracy in the 21st century: from the managed to the entrepreneurial economy, *Journal of Evolutionary, 10(1), p.17-34.*

Begley, T.M. & Boyd, D.P. (1987), *"Psychological characteristics associated with performance in entrepreneurial firms and smaller businesses"*, Journal of Business Venturing, 2, 79-93.

Brinkman, E. (2000), *Research about success- and failfactors of starters,* Masterthesis, RUG.

Brockhaus, Sr., R.H. (1982), "The psychology of the entrepreneur", in: Encyclopaedia of Entrepreneurship, 39-57, Englewood Cliffs, New Jersey.

Ciavarella, M.A., Buckholtz, A.K., Riordan, C.M., Gatewood, R.D. and G.S. Stokes (2004), *"The BIG FIVE and venture survival: Is there a linkage?* Journal of Business Venturing, 19, p. 465-483

Driessen, M.P. (2005), E-Scan Ondernemerstest, beoordeling en ontwikkeling ondernemerscompetentie, Dissertatie RUG, Groningen.

Flier, van den J. (1990), *Verslag van een praktijktest van de BSOK,* Instituut Midden en Kleinbedrijf, Hoofddorp.

Gelderen, M.W. van, Thurik, A.R., & Bosma, N. (2005), Success and risk factors in the pre startup phase. *Small Business Economics*, 24, 4, 365-380.

Hmieleski, K.M. and A.C. Corbett (2006), *"Proclivity for improvisation as a predictor of entrepreneurial intentions"*, Journal of Small Business Management, vol. 44, nr. 1, pp. 45-63.

Herrmann, N. (1996), The whole brain business book, McGraw-Hill, New York

Hoekstra, H.A., Ormel, J. & Fruyt, F. de (1993), *Handboek Neo PI-R en Neo FFI,* Swets en Zeitlinger.

Jung, C.G. (1923), *Psychological types,* New York, Harcourt Brace

Lahti, R.K. (1999), "Identifying and Integrating Individual Level and Organizational Level Core Competencies", *Journal of Business and Psychology,* vol. 14, 1, p 59-75.

Lorrain, J & Dussault, L. (1988Grant, Paul & Perren, Lew (.2002).Small business and entrepreneurial research: meta-theories, paradigms and prejudices. International Small Business Journal, 20(2).

Hisrich, R & Drnovsek, M. (2002).Entrepreneurship and small business research-a European perspective. Journal of Small Business and Enterprise Development9 (2).

Hisrich, R. & Drnovsek, M. (2002). Entrepreneurship and small business research – a European perspective. Journal of Small Business and Enterprise Development 9 (2).

Mare, G.F. (1996). A manual for Entrepreneurship: The road to a successful career. Pretoria, Kagiso Uitgewers.

Nieuwenhuizen, C. (Ed). (2004). Basics of Entrepreneurship. Juta: Pretoria

Kotler, P, Armstrong, G. (2000). Marketing an Introduction, 5th edition. New Jersey: Prentice Hall.

Saunders, M, Thornhill, A & Lewis, P. (2009). Research Methods for Students. 5th edition. Harlow: FT/Prentice Hall.

Shajahan Dr.S (.2004).Research Methods forManagement.2nd Ed, India: Jaico Publishing house.

Zukmund, W.G. (2003) .Business Research Method.7th Ed.Uncinnati, OH: Thomson Publishing.

WITHDRAWN

Made in the USA
Charleston, SC
14 October 2014